Rosa Parks

A Buddy Book
by
Sarah Tieck

ABDO
Publishing Company

VISIT US AT

www.abdopublishing.com

Published by ABDO Publishing Company, 4940 Viking Drive, Suite 622, Edina, Minnesota 55435. Copyright © 2007 by Abdo Consulting Group, Inc. International copyrights reserved in all countries. No part of this book may be reproduced in any form without written permission from the publisher.

Printed in the United States.

Contributing Editor: Michael P. Goecke
Graphic Design: Jane Halbert
Cover Photograph: Library of Congress
Interior Photographs/Illustrations: Hulton Archives, Library of Congress, North Wind, Photodisc

Library of Congress Cataloging-in-Publication Data

Tieck, Sarah, 1976–
   Rosa Parks / Sarah Tieck.
      p. cm. — (First biographies. Set V.)
   Includes index.
   ISBN 10 1-59679-788-6
   ISBN 13 978-1-59679-788-8
   1. Parks, Rosa, 1913—Juvenile literature. 2. African American women—Alabama—Montgomery—Biography—Juvenile literature. 3. African Americans—Alabama—Montgomery—Biography—Juvenile literature. 4. Civil rights workers—Alabama—Montgomery—Biography—Juvenile literature. 5. African Americans—Civil rights—Alabama—Montgomery—History—20th century—Juvenile literature. 6. Segregation in transportation—Alabama—Montgomery—History—20th century—Juvenile literature. 7. Montgomery (Ala.)—Race relations—Juvenile literature. 8. Montgomery (Ala.)—Biography—Juvenile literature. I. Title II. Series: Gosda, Randy T, 1959- . First biographies. Set V.

F334.M753P3884 2006
323.092—dc22

                                                                2005031971

Table Of Contents

Who Is Rosa Parks?

Rosa Parks was a famous African-American woman.

Rosa Parks was known for her courage. She had an important role in the Civil Rights Movement. She was one of the first people to fight segregation.

Some people call Rosa Parks the "Mother of the Civil Rights Movement."

Rosa's Family

Rosa Parks was born in Tuskegee, Alabama, on February 4, 1913. At that time, her name was Rosa McCauley.

Rosa's mother was Leona McCauley. Rosa's father was James McCauley. Rosa had a younger brother named Sylvester.

Alabama is in the southern part of the United States.

Rosa's family was poor. Her father left when she was very little. She only saw him a couple of times during her childhood. Rosa's mother had to work to take care of Rosa and her brother.

Growing Up

Rosa, her mother, and her brother lived with Rosa's grandparents. They had a small farm in Pine Level, Alabama. Rosa and Sylvester liked to play in the pine tree woods around Pine Level. They'd splash in the creeks and ponds and play outside. Rosa liked to play hide-and-seek.

Rosa went to school in a one-room schoolhouse. She liked to learn. Rosa's mother thought education was very important. She said learning would help Rosa build a better life. Rosa's school was only for African-American children.

This one-room schoolhouse is similar to the school Rosa attended.

Rosa's church was right next to her school. Church was important to Rosa and her family. They attended the Mount Zion African Methodist Episcopal Church.

An Unfriendly World

Rosa grew up in a time when African Americans were not treated the same as white people. Rosa and other African Americans often suffered from racial discrimination. Rosa went to a school just for African-American children. She was not allowed to go to school with white children. This kind of racial discrimination was common before the Civil Rights Movement.

As a little girl, Rosa was afraid of the Ku Klux Klan. The Ku Klux Klan was a group of people who dressed in white hoods and cloaks. Its members didn't like people who were different than them. They didn't like African Americans. The Ku Klux Klan rode around at night. Sometimes Klan members would burn down houses. They hurt and killed many African-American people.

The Ku Klux Klan burned down many houses.

Rosa's grandfather would watch for the Ku Klux Klan at night. He wanted to keep his family safe. Sometimes Rosa would watch with him. Many nights, Rosa and Sylvester slept in their clothes. That way, if the Ku Klux Klan came, they could run and hide.

Ku Klux Klan members wore white robes and hoods to hide their identities.

Rosa realized African Americans were treated differently. She wanted to help make the world safe for African Americans.

Leaving Home

Rosa's school only went up to the sixth grade. In 1924, when she turned 11, she moved to Montgomery, Alabama. She attended the Montgomery Industrial School for Girls. Later, Rosa returned to Pine Level to help take care of her sick grandmother.

Rosa married Raymond Parks on December 18, 1932. Raymond was a barber. He was interested in civil rights.

Rosa and Raymond lived in Montgomery for many years. Rosa graduated from high school in 1934. Later, she attended the Alabama State Teachers College.

This group of women includes NAACP members.

In Montgomery, Rosa worked as a seamstress. Also, she was the secretary for the Montgomery Chapter of the National Association for the Advancement of Colored People (NAACP). She was one of the first women to join.

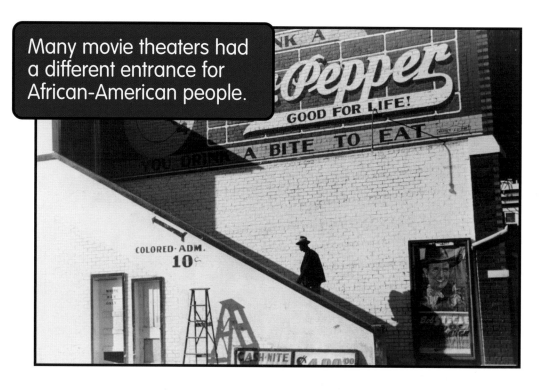

Many movie theaters had a different entrance for African-American people.

Rosa and Raymond often noticed unfairness against African Americans. They wanted African Americans to be treated like all United States citizens.

Fighting Segregation

Segregation laws were common in the South. Montgomery had many segregation laws. One law banned African Americans from sitting at the front of city buses. Only

white citizens could sit in those seats. Rosa thought segregation was unfair.

African-American people had to drink water from different drinking fountains.

Rosa was arrested because she wouldn't give up her seat on a bus.

Rosa rode the city bus to and from work. One day, a bus driver asked Rosa to give her seat to a white person. She said no. So, the police arrested her.

A police officer fingerprinted Rosa after she was arrested.

The Civil Rights Movement

Rosa's courage led to the Montgomery city bus boycott. Many African-American people stopped riding Montgomery's city buses. A boycott is when many people agree not to use something. A boycott sends a message. It shows that people think something is wrong.

One of Rosa's friends was a man named Dr. Martin Luther King, Jr. Dr. King became famous for leading the Civil Rights Movement. He fought for

Dr. Martin Luther King, Jr.

rights for African Americans. Like Rosa, Dr. King thought segregation was wrong.

On April 26, 1956, Dr. King told people he would continue the bus boycott. People cheered.

After the bus boycott began, Dr. King helped to keep it going. He and some other people formed the Montgomery Improvement Association on December 5, 1955. This group wanted to fight segregation laws. Soon, African Americans joined the bus boycott. This boycott lasted for more than one year.

In 1956, the United States Supreme Court said that Montgomery's bus law was wrong. The boycott had worked.

Many things changed after the bus boycott. Rosa's brave act had helped make things better for African Americans. This was a very important moment in United States history.

Dr. King (second seat to the left) rode the bus after the Supreme Court ruling.

A Lasting Legacy

After the bus boycott, Rosa lost her job as a seamstress. But, she and Raymond continued to help in the fight for civil rights. This made many people angry. Some of them wanted to hurt Rosa. She and Raymond moved to Detroit, Michigan, in 1957. There they could continue their work.

Rosa (left) with Eleanor Roosevelt (middle) and Mrs. H.C. Foster at a civil rights rally in New York City.

In 1977, Raymond died. Rosa was very sad, but she continued to work. She opened the Rosa and Raymond Parks Institute for Self Development in 1987. In 1992, she wrote a book about her life. It is called *Rosa Parks: My Story*.

Over the years, Rosa won many awards. In 1996, Rosa received the Presidential Medal of Freedom.

Rosa lived in Detroit until her death at 92. Rosa Parks died on October 24, 2005. After Rosa died, her body laid overnight in the United States Capitol Rotunda. This is a special honor. Rosa is the first woman to receive this honor.

Rosa Parks worked for many years to make life better for African Americans. Today, segregation laws don't exist or are unconstitutional. Rosa Parks helped make many changes. She is remembered as an important American for her work in the Civil Rights Movement.

President Bill Clinton gave Rosa Parks the Presidential Medal of Frededom in 1996.

Important Dates

February 4, 1913 Rosa Parks is born.

1924 Rosa moves to Montgomery to go to school.

December 18, 1932 Rosa marries Raymond Parks.

1943 Rosa works as a secretary for the National Association for the Advancement of Colored People (NAACP) in Montgomery.

December 1, 1955 Rosa does not give up her seat on a bus.

December 5, 1955 The Montgomery city bus boycott begins. It will last 382 days.

December 20, 1956 The bus boycott ends. The United States Supreme Court says that segregation on public transportation is unconstitutional.

1957 Rosa and Raymond move to Detroit, Michigan.

1977 Raymond dies.

1987 Rosa opens the Rosa and Raymond Parks Institute for Self Development.

1992 Rosa publishes *Rosa Parks: My Story*.

February 4, 2005 Rosa celebrates her 92nd birthday in Detroit, Michigan.

October 24, 2005 Rosa Parks dies.

Important Words

African American an American whose family
members came from Africa.

civil rights equal rights for all citizens.

Civil Rights Movement a public fight for civil rights
for all people.

racial discrimination the act of treating someone
unfairly based on their skin color or race.

segregation laws that separate African Americans
from white people.

unconstitutional something that does not agree
with the constitution.

Web Sites

To learn more about Rosa Parks, visit ABDO Publishing
Company on the World Wide Web. Web site links about
Rosa Parks are featured on our Book Links page. These
links are routinely monitored and updated to provide the
most current information available.

www.abdopublishing.com

Index